A Masterpiece of Poetry

A Masterpiece of Poetry

Author: Roger Cosby
Co-Author: Dr. Kathleen Cosby-Tabb

Library of Congress Control Number:		2021902829
ISBN:	Hardcover	978-1-6641-5756-9
	Softcover	978-1-6641-5755-2
	eBook	978-1-6641-5754-5

All images are from Pixabay.

Print information available on the last page.

Rev. date: 02/22/2021

To order additional copies of this book, contact:
Xlibris
844-714-8691
www.Xlibris.com
Orders@Xlibris.com
825546

Amazon
Barnes & Noble

Author's Website:
www.newworldpoet.org

Co-Author's Website:
https://www.drkathleencosbytabb.com/

CONTENTS

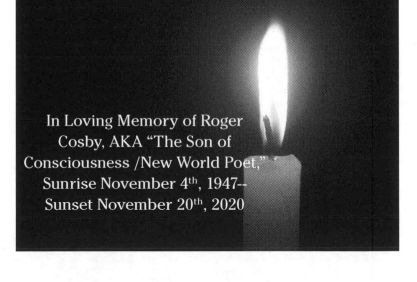

In Loving Memory of Roger Cosby, AKA "The Son of Consciousness /New World Poet," Sunrise November 4th, 1947-- Sunset November 20th, 2020

1.

My Bequeath

I offer you a drink from my spirit,
you who aspire the champion's dream
I offer you a drink from my spirit,
you who aspire the champion's throne
I offer you the dragon's heart,
you who wish slavery to depart
I offer you the poet's tongue,
you who wish to remove Social wrong
I offer you the stateman's mind,
you who wish to challenge time
I offer you the dancer's grace,
you who wish to fly away!

2.

BROTHER

Burden bearer of the weak, friend to the strong
Carved out of rock, spirit hewn out of stone
Merciful and compassionate; wise in your steps
Prone to love and help
One in a thousand, will walk in your steps
One in a thousand, will pass your test
Brother

3.

I Exist Because God Exists!

I have no existence, I can proclaim:
I am born not of myself
My existence is because of the existence of God
I am a thought, in the realm of God's imagination,
And the rock, the bird, the bee, all that I see,
is of the nature of me
...A mere thought of God!

4.

My Name is Destiny

I watched you in the playground,
you were different from all the rest
I followed your footsteps across the sands of time
And nature so swiftly raised you
from childhood to manhood
When demons of darkness treaded on your path...
I shook them to their knees -
I was your guardian angel, you see
My Name is Destiny
I planted the seed in young soil,
and they had no will of their own
They fulfilled my plan and made me proud
My name is Destiny

5.

THE IMPOSSIBLE

Searching for the impossible
Earth's plane offers no more
Reality and I stand toe to toe
To do the impossible is my prayer
Defying odds is glory most vain
One must search for the impossible things
But Earth's plane makes no yield
Reality here, is reality for real

6.

Do You believe?

Ask yourself for the power to be
And chase the rainbow to its' lofty heights
And lose, not your will to fight
And say to the wind "Peace Be Still"
And walk the water with no learned skill
Do you believe?
Then, free yourself from flesh and bones
And give your spirit the freedom to roam
And sink never to the pit of doubt
Forever, be a child birthed by belief, power and might
Do you believe?

7.

FATE...

Inescapable dreams of the Cosmic machine
Appointments made before I was conceived
Hills I would either climb or fall down
Games I would win... Games I would loose
Songs I would sing, fears I would shed
Inescapable dreams of the Cosmic machine
Appointments in time,
buried in the consciousness of my mind

8.

EMPTINESS

Awaken from your sleep, great soul in me
I want to feel the beauty of life
And touch your morning lips
Awaken from your sleep, great soul in me
I want to blend with the night
And bend with the Sunset

9.

PEACE

Greater than silver, I knew you to be
I treaded the mountains to see your face
You stood high above the turmoil of the human race

Wisdom himself stood at your guard
and no flesh could touch your lofty parts
Wisdom beckoned me to your feet
I kneeled in humanity to your presence - most sweet

And greater than silver, I knew you to be
I walked on your mountain, I knelled at your feet
They told me, your name was Peace

10.

LOST SOULS

Lost souls, lost souls travelling on the wrong road…
Don't you see the end of your journey?
Don't you see the damnation?
Don't you see your destination?
Don't you hear heaven calling your name?
Don't you see the devil's game
Lost souls, lost souls travelling on the wrong road…
Your Heavenly Father wants to bathe you in His love
Your Heavenly Father wants to hold you in His arms
Lost souls, lost souls travelling on the wrong road…

11.

I Am a Believer

Because I am a Believer,
no stone on my path cannot be overturned
The mountain hears my footsteps
and moves out of my way
The infidels see me coming and run to the hills
We fear the believer; their voices squealed
Because I am a believer, my powers are great!
Sixteen dragons flee me, yet none of them escape
Because I am a Believer
I roam highways, where darkness will not tread
I know no hunger from life... I am fed
Because I am a Believer

12.

NO QUITTER

Call Me No Quitter
I must challenge - I must contend
I must express, the God within
But, call me no quitter
All the insults, I have borne well
and the poison of my enemy's tongue
...I can still smell
But, call me no quitter
My heart burns with a vigor to be
My soul roams in the darkness of the night
Seeking new dreams, to bring to the light
But, call me no quitter

13.

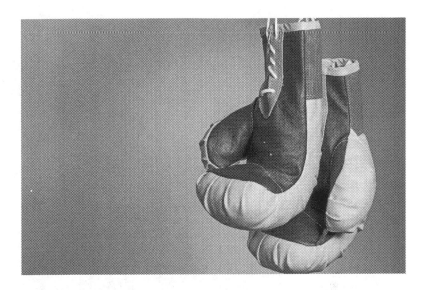

FIGHT LIKE A CHAMP...

Cast fear to the tide,
deliver your punches with great power
Fight like a Champ... young man, young woman
This is your day by God's will challenge
The contention with boast and bravery
And up you will rise, from life's slavery

This is your day by God's will
take your shot and make your kill
But, fight like a Champ...
And in the fifteenth round, when all is said and done
You will walk away with the crown and feel no dread
Fight like a Champ... young man, young woman
Fight like a Champ...

14.

FEAR

Grand Warden of the spirit, soul and mind
Taskmaster of beast, foul and mankind
Robber of all attributes; high and low
Product of ignorance, impacting one's ability to grow
Great thief in man's darkest night…
Killer of courage and will;
what spirit today did you come to steal?

15.

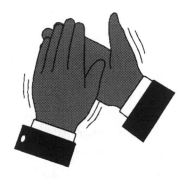

GIVE YOURSELF
A HAND...

Give yourself a hand; black folks!
Give yourself a hand...
Superman aint got nothing on you
Rise and break your chains
Get ready to wear your crown
Because the justice of heaven is coming down
Give yourself a hand; black folks!
You are a people Supreme
Superman aint got nothing on you
The noble lion of the jungle
In all of his glory, cries human tears
If he knows your story
Give yourself a hand; black folks!
Give yourself a hand...
Superman aint got nothing on you
Give yourself a hand...

16.

Keep it Moving

Keep it moving, keep it moving
Sometimes your faith is going to
take you to the mountain top
And sometimes your fear is going to
bring you to the bottom
Keep it moving, keep it moving

Sometimes friends from long ago,
will stop knocking on your door
Sometimes the love that once made you glad,
is now going to make you sad
Sometimes in life,
the boss man is going to give you a pink slip
And you are not going to be able to pay your rent
Keep it moving, keep it moving

The sunshine is on its' way
And you will have some more beautiful days
The rain is about to fall and flowers
are going to rise up in your garden
Keep it moving, keep it moving
There is a mighty blessing waiting on you up ahead
If you don't let your faith grow dead
Keep it moving, keep it moving

THE SPEED OF LIGHT
(dedicated to Muhammad Ali)

Moving at the Speed of Light
Jabs are shooting from left to right
Up high on my toes
Beautiful, beautiful prose
Traveling like a train, through the tracks of my mind
Traveling like a train, by the power of my brain
A punch-drunk boxer, I could never be
Moving too fast for the eyes to see.

18.

REDEMPTION
(dedicated to Muhammad Ali)

How did I end up on this deck?
Joe Frazier, is standing over my chest
I must summon the power of self
I am who told the world, I am the best
My legs must obey my command...
Success will be mine, in the last stand
Heart must obey my command...
Will must obey my command...
Champion, Champion, Champion, Man!

I Ride My Thoughts
(dedicated to Muhammad Ali)

I ride on thoughts, I rumble on the ropes
I hide my face in the rope-a-dope,
I ride my thoughts, I rumble on the ropes
I dance to the rhythm of Black folks
I ride my thoughts, I speak my mind
I call my victory in any round.

20.

EGYPT UNDER MY FEET

My mind commanded you to exist
My feet walked upon your soil
You were my mothership
I was your captain
I populated all of Africa
I returned to you from alien soil
I saw my face, in the face of your Pharaoh
I saw my genes, in the face of your Queen
I saw my soul, in the mystery of your pyramid
Your soul was sweet under my feet!

21.

MOTHER AFRICA

When the most High created you in ancient times,
He put gold underneath your feet...
He put wisdom in your mind...
He put diamonds on your head...
He put love in your soul...
He put beauty in your face...
He made you the goddess of the human race---

My mother, your mother, Mother Africa
I heard your cry--- an historic cry
Because your children had been stolen and enslaved
In many nations, in many cultures, in many civilizations
I heard you Mother Africa-call them back home

22.

GRANDPA SAID...

Grandpa sat back in his rocking chair
He said, "Billy Boy- Joe, you come near
He said,
"I'm going to tell you a story about Father Time
And how things in life really go down"
He said Father Time is the keeper of truth...
The maker of wisdom and the giver of youth
He said that when the Good Lord
made heaven and earth
Father Time was there, before he made the dirt
He said when the Good Lord told the winds to blow
The mountains to rise, and the oceans to flow
He said Father Time already knew,
what the Lord was going to do
He said before the Good Lord made the stars to shine
The rain to fall,
the moon to glow and the human mind...
He had already made Father Time

23.

DIGNITY DOES NOT DIE

They called him Dignity and Dignity does not die
Though underneath a slave's feet
He sometimes takes a long sleep
But Dignity does not die
Though underneath the vanquished heels
He sometimes seems flimsy and unreal
But Dignity does not die

JUSTICE

When the rich man's justice in the society of man
Is greater than the poor man's justice
The heart of Almighty God is not pleased
And justice herself will cry out in the night
For a Savior to come to redeem her righteous soul
To place her noble crown back upon her noble head
So that justice in the society of man…shall not be dead

25.

THE JUDGEMENT

What is the judgement my Brotherman?
It is the bread that you casted upon the water?
It is the justice that you gave to your social order?
It is the prayers that you did or did not make unto God?

The judgment, my man...
is the total of your rights and wrongs
Revisited upon you in the physical form
The judgement, my man...is the beauty of your soul
...Expressed in wisdom and sculpted in gold
The judgment is you, me,
the sum total of all compassion
...And all cries

26.

Dancing Girl!

Dancing to the stars, up in the sky
Dancing to the dreams, that will never die
Dancing for the souls, that forgot how to cry
Dancing girl! --- Dancing girl!
Dancing for peace, to be mankind's quest
Dancing for justice, to speak his truth
Dancing for salvation, for today's youth
Dancing girl! --- Dancing girl!
Going to the house of broken dreams
Keeping her faith and love in all human beings
Sitting at the feet of father time
Pouring his wisdom into her mind
Hearing the righteous cry of a prophet of love
For more justice in our world
Dancing girl! --- Dancing girl!
You dance till Christ's spirt rises in the land
And make all folks love their fellow man
You dance till Dr. King's dream rises and shines
And bring love and justice to all mankind
Dancing girl! ---Dancing girl!

27.

FAKE GOD'S

Fake God's, fake God's bring pain and sorrow
Traveling in a fate reality, living in a false mentality
Worshipping superficially
Separated from divine morality
Who is that boy, who is that man?
Who is that lady, eating out of the trash can?
Fake God's, fake God's-Satan is buying and selling souls
Just like he did, in days of old
The souls of nations the Devils own
Just like he did, in the days of Rome
Fake God's bring pain and sorrow
Heavens throne destroyed Rome
Sodom and Gomorrah and Babylon too

Fake God's, fake God's-bring pain and sorrow
Fake God's will lead you astray
and a great price you will have to pay
On Judgement day

28.

SOMETIMES

Sometimes the wind doesn't blow
Sometimes the rain doesn't show
Sometimes the sun doesn't shine
Sometimes a friend you can't find
But there is somebody in the world above,
Who you can call on day or night
...And he will talk to you about your problems of life

Sometimes in life, you just can't win
Sometimes the journey gets so hard
But there is somebody in the world above
Who will never deny you his grace or his love

He is the King of Kings, and the Lord of Lords
When he speaks, the thunder must listen
The rain must fall, the saints must stand tall
There is no problem great or small
That he cannot help you when you call.

FAMILY

Acorns of the same tree...
Carrying the tide of the wind
Blades of grass, flourishing on fertile black soil
Vessels filled with the wine
of mothers' and fathers' youthful desires
Multiple roots tied to the knots of humanity
Acorns of the same tree...
Faces filled with diversity; individuality bursting to be

30.

HERO LOVE...

We seek a soul like our own
We dare a dream to be born
We grope in the darkness for a new thought
Our heroes are born of the justice we crave
From the pain of our souls, their lives are made
We ride the waves of history most swift
In the society of man, we bow to our debts
But our heroes, we cherish above the rest

31.

Gotta Go Make the Donuts

Gotta go make the donuts… I know, I know
Gotta go make the donuts…you go, you go
I am on the night train, got stress in my brain
It's a two-job thang
Landlord knocking on my door
He says, "Give me my rent…
Or you and your daughters gotta go"
Gotta go make the donuts… I know, I know
Gotta go make the donuts… you go, you go
Is this a nightmare or is it a sweet dream?
Where some people win and some people cry
Or some people live and some people die
Gotta go make the donuts… I know, I know
Gotta go make the donuts… you go, you go
I feel like I gotta forty-four pistol
Up against my head
Every time somebody knocks on my door,
I think it's the landlord coming for his bread
Gotta go make the donuts, I know, I know

32.

CHURCH LADY

Sister good sister, is a good old soul
So her life story should be told
She goes to church on Sunday,
rolls all over the church floor
But her mind is on triple 9's
She says, "if she hits it, she's gonna live real fine
She says it would be great, if she could just hit 268
She would put some real money in the preacher's plate

Sister...good sister, don't you know -
the devil is laughing behind your back
He says that he got you hooked on gambling;
maybe he can get you hooked on crack
Sister...good sister, don't you know
that God doesn't want you giving Him
Or the church any of the Devil's dough

ANGELS IN THE BLUE

Angels in the flesh, dragons against death
You got my love, you got my respect
Angels in the blue, watching out for you
Heroes in the night, heroes in the day
When the sun goes down and the eyes go to sleep
And death comes a calling, like a mean old creep
There will be angels in the blue, watching over you

Keep them in your prayers, by night and by day
Because down into the mouth of death,
they walk each day
Time is the enemy and death is moving fast
Move out of their way y'all,
when you hear the sirens come past
Angels in the blue, watching over me and you

34.

Not Going There

I'm not going to go there any more
I'm not going to go there again, my friend
I've been to the place called broken Hartville
In a time in life, when I thought everything was real
I thought Peter Pan was a real man
I thought Superman could really fly
I thought Batman could walk up walls
I thought flowers grew seventeen feet tall
This time, I'm going to wait on the real thang
I'm going to find me a righteous woman
and give her my name
I'm going to make us some babies and build us a home
I'm going to walk in the footsteps of Jesus Christ
And live a good and Godly life
I'm not going to go there again, my friend

35.

PHILADELPHIA

She is standing tall-a historic land that welcomes all
We got Love Park, we got the Liberty Bell
We got hundreds of years of history here
We got people reaching their dreams,

We got some mighty fine human beings,
here in Philadelphia
We got Rocky's statute at the Museum
We got Joe Frazier's historic boxing gym
We are blessed to have had
Marian Anderson, John Coltrane, Chubby Checker,
Frankie Avalon, Billy Paul, Paul Robeson,

Phyllis Hyman, Dr. J., Pete Rose and Wilt Chamberlain
Philadelphia, Philadelphia, Philadelphia
Like all cities, we done had some pain...
But on the scale of history, we have a good name!

36.

I PROMISE

You were in my mornings and I was in your evenings
You were in my footstep and I was in your heart beat
Then, time came and took away our sunshine
Then, time came and took loves smile
Then, time came and stole loves dreams
Then, time came back and bowed his noble knees
And said… he was sorry for the universe's deeds
Then hope came and said, "I will not let your love die
And this I promise to all the stars in the sky"

37.

HOME

Here I will stake my claim
Build my hut, plant my roots
A wanderer, I will be no more
I take this Earth as my home
...To feed my body and rest my bones

38.

WALKING ON WATER

Sometimes you gotta walk on water, to have a friend
Sometimes you gotta walk on water, if you want to win
I'm walking on water to keep my dreams
I'm walking on water to be a great human being
I went down into the valley of the shadow of death
And I called on the Lord to give me some help
Then, a voice cried out from the Heaven's above
You gotta walk on water, to find your dreams
You gotta walk on water, to be a great human being
My spirit, my faith and my soul is walking on water
If you want to wear the Golden crown,
you gotta walk on water and don't go down

39.

A PHONE CALL

I got a phone call last night
From somebody I had fought
We said some things that were not nice
We said some things that came from our pain
We said some things that made each other feel shame
I got a phone call last night
And a voice from deep in somebody's soul
Said, I forgive you, I forgive you...
and I need you to forgive me
I need you and I need you to need me
I miss you and I hope you miss me too
I still love you and I hope you still love me
I got a phone call last night...

40

KEEP SMILING

Don't let Satan take your smile
Just remember you are still God's child
And heaven got your back
Heaven is only one prayer away
Whether, it's a sunshiny or rainy day
I know you been walking down roads
that have no lights
I know you been fighting some battles
in your soul and in your life
But, don't let Satan take your smile
because the Heaven's got your back
So, get up in the morning and fall to your knees
and ask God for the power
To be what you want to be,
and don't let the Devil take your smile
Because you are still God's child
and Heaven's got your back

41.

POLLUTION

The white birds don't fly to the oceans no more
To feed their babies from the waters below
They come to the cities to cry for bread
Because the pollution of man is killing them dead
The polar bear is fighting for his life
Because the fire from the snow is melting his ice

The ozone is crying in the heavens above
Because man-made pollution is killing her world
And if the ozone goes, all is going to die
In a great big ball of cosmic fire
Mother Nature is talking to us
She says the question is and always has been---
Do you want her to be your enemy
or do you want her to be your friend?

42.

SANTA CLAUSE

I saw Santa Clause down at the welfare office
He said he needs some money for donuts and coffee
He said the Momma's and Poppa's are crying the blues
Because they don't have no money
To buy their kids no toys or shoes
He said Rudolph didn't have anything to eat
And all of his reindeer were about ready to weep
He said Rudolph, Rudolph please don't cry
Cause Uncle Sam is going to cut us a piece of the pie
I saw the big guy hook up his sleigh
He said, he was going back to the North Pole
to count his bread
Before someone shoots him and his reindeer dead
Life in the city is just too cold
People killing people and losing their soul
He said when is man going to learn?
That they cannot solve their problems
from a barrel of a gun
He said run Rudolph, run, he said run Rudolph, run

43.

FANTASY WINGS

My dreams are my wings
They let me be, who I want to be
They let me travel in unlimited space and time
They give me faith, they give me power

My dreams are my wings
They make me rise and stand tall
They make me believe I can do it all
They make me reach for the stars
They make me love from the heart
They give me new hope, when old hope dies
They make me believe, I can fly
My dreams are my wings

44.

PUNKHOOD

Punkhood... don't give you no manhood
Twenty-five young people doing a beat down
On another human being, down on the ground
Another video, another movie being made
And another sad day for the human race
I hear a wicked mouth in a crowd of folks
Disrespecting another human being -
just to make a joke

Punkhood... don't give you no power
Punkhood... is just the way of a coward
If you want some manhood,
show some love to all mankind
Show some love to the Word of God
Show some love to a blind woman or man
Show some love to anybody you can
Because Punkhood... don't give you no manhood

45.

Punks in the Hood (Continued)

Punks in the hood trying to be men
Too scared to love, too scared to live
Give a punk in the hood some love

I never had any love, I never had any respect
I call my own self a nigger
that should tell you I'm ignorant
I do drive by shootings, just to get attention
I sell drugs on the corner,
to put some gold around my neck
It takes away my pain, it gives me a rep
I been to the jail house, it ain't nothing but a zoo
It transforms you, into an animal too

I wear a mask on my face, to hide my shame
In my prison cell, is where I spend most of my time
I pull off my mask and I break down
Punks in the hood trying to be men
Ain't got no woman, ain't got no friend
Give a punk in the hood some love y'all
Give a punk in the hood some love y'all

46.

SISTER COOL-GURL

Sister Cool-Gurl, that guy ain't got
no ring on your finger
And he is using what you got down below
For nothing, but a playground-don't you know
Your Momma done told you to stay in school
And don't let a pretty faced boy, play you for a fool
Life outside, ain't no joke
When the rent man come knocking on your door,
And the boss man tells you
he doesn't need you no more

Sister Cool-Gurl, your momma done
told you about life's rules
Education is a passport to a better tomorrow
So, stay in school and don't be nobody's fool
You can do badly, all by yourself
You don't need five or six babies and nobody to help
Sister Cool-Gurl remember, mother birds
build themselves a nest
Before she lays her eggs,
so her baby chicks will have somewhere to
Lay their head

47.

POVERTY AND POWER

I've seen poverty
I've seen power
My feet have tread both paths
And destiny ruled, which I was to have
I have known the hunger of the Ghetto child
I have had the power of the rich and the wild
I've seen poverty
I've seen power from the King of nothing
to the King of All
How fickle be the grace of fate?

48.

I Heard My People Cry

It came to my ears from the streets of Alabama
And the super gold halls of justice
I heard my people cry
My back could not turn against the cry of my people
So, I took my stand against injustice...
and any oppression throughout the land
I would not be a slave, fool or tool
I stood for justice by the rule
I heard my people cry; I did take my stand...
destined not to be an Uncle Tom, Man

49.

BROKEN

The wings of my dreams are broken
My hope is dead
And there are no good thoughts in my head
Does anyone in the house know God's phone number?
Can you talk louder? Sir, did you say its 1-800 Prayer?

50.

PLANTATION NIGGERS

Plantation Niggers are quick to pull the trigger
They don't kill nothing,
but their own brothers and sisters
Black folks need you to vanish from the planet earth
So that they can lift themselves out of the dirt
Plantation Niggers quick to pull the trigger
Plantation Niggers, don't have any love for themselves
They are looking for knowledge of mankind
In gangster rap and rhyme
Plantation Niggers are quick
to pull the trigger on their own people
In their own ignorance, they think they are free
If they can wear a piece of gold around their neck,
after they sell crack
To their own brothers and sisters
Their enemy they would like to be;
that's why their own greatness, they cannot see
Plantation Niggers are quick to pull the trigger
But they don't kill nothing,
but their own brothers and sisters
Slave Master John controls their mind

51.

MAN TO MAN

Give me my reparations and give them to me now
I hear the ancestors calling from the grave
They say go tell the president-you gotta get paid
They say from the plantation to the ghetto, is no justice
They say 40-acres and a mule do you better
I've been to the mountain top
and I saw the promised-land
Black folks had lots of money;
Black folks had lots of land
I made you America, the God of the nations
By giving you America 400 years of free slave labor
You give trillions of dollars, to foreign nations
Then, you look at me like I'm crazy -
when I ask for my reparations
The government said after slavery was over
Black folks could have 40 acres
and a mule to start all over
Then you had a change of heart and a change of plan
Then you sent Black folks
from the plantation to the Ghetto land
Give me my reparations

52.

MANDELA MAN

Come to the house of my dreams
And I will sing you a song
that will make you love freedom all night long
I am traveling on a Freedom train
flowing through the soul
Looking for a place, they call Freedom Road
I'm traveling the speed of light in the day, in the night
I'm speaking freedom truth to the human mind
I'm speaking freedom love to all mankind
I'm giving freedom and hope to a billion souls
I'm giving freedom and hope to the young and the old
I am a Mandela Man

53.

OPRAH

Mother Nature had a great day,
when she gave Oprah to the human race
And a queen walked out of time,
to inspire and to uplift all mankind
She heard the children crying in the Motherland
To have an education in the society of man
She stood on the waters down in New Orleans
And said we gotta help these suffering human beings
She went down to Haiti and looked death in the face
And said you cannot destroy the human race
She spoke her voice in the streets of our land
And said, "Folks, you gotta stop hating your fellow man"

54.

My Name is Love

A hungry child in a Mississippi town
Rock bottom poor and falling to the ground
Mother done gone, Father don't care
from such a condition, I cannot abstain
I am a creature, who must respond to pain
A drunkard gray haired old man on a Harlem doorstep...
Too weak to die; can't escape the darkness of his life
A broken-down ex-hooker on a Chicago street
So washed up, so utterly beat
The best years passing
and no dreams in the future to be had
I am giving her one last ounce of hope
A brand-new baby, just brought to life
I am his host on his first night
And during his years,
I'll be there in all his dread and in his despair
I am the blood of his body and the spirit of his bones
...My name is Love

55.

NATIONAL ANTHEM
FOR THE HOMELESS

I am the you, but could be me
I am the me, but could be you
I am the man; I am the woman
I am the child, which has no home to call my own
I am the you, but could be me
I am the me, but could be you
…Waiting for humanity to embrace me with love and
compassion

56.

Unzip and Zip

Unzip your brain son
You think sex is a joke
You think babies are a hoax
You think procreation is a playground
You think society won't shoot you down
Zip up your pants son
Unzip your brain boy...
Sex is something sacred, sex is not a toy

57.

SMOKING GUN

Justice is weeping, love is sleeping
And peace done took another vacation
And the gun is still smoking
And twenty- five bullets
are in a young black man's back
And the spirit of hate in America, is stacked
And somewhere in this old town
Another black Momma has tears in her eyes
A broken heart and a dead child
And a black Poppa is frozen in grief
With a sad spirit and a tongue, that cannot speak
And somewhere in the house of the Lord
A Black preacher is preaching;
to find some faith that will make love rise,

Make hate die and stop the black race
from losing their mind
And the gun is still smoking
And out in the graveyard,
black folks come to say goodbye
To another young black man, who racism crucified
And the grave diggers, are shaking their heads
As they open up the earth---
for another young black man to lay his head
And the gun is still smoking, smoking, smoking

58.

I QUESTION...

What is this thing that we call life?
A dream, a drama, a divine scheme?
Or maybe just a cosmic machine?
So mathematical, so divine
How could it be?
It's a beauty... we do not see
We are earthly creatures of laughter and jest
self-righteous idiots, at our very best

But my friend-what is this thing called life?
Atoms and molecules the scientist would say
Spirits and flesh, if you ask the preacher
Games and sweet things to the little kids, as they play
Dollars and cents to the merchant man
Peace and love to the musician clan
What is this thing called life?
Heaven and Hell, I heard an old soul say
A search for truth to the Monk and Guru

Indeed, my friends it is all of these things
But mostly it is just sweet, sweet dreams

59.

UNKNOWN

Nobody knows my name
But I'm so good at my game
But nobody, but nobody, knows my name

I write my poetry in solitude
I sing my blues on the roof tops of the town
I play my trumpet down by the lake
And only the birds listen to my melodies
Nobody, nobody, knows my name
But I'm so good at my game
I feel sometimes like a ghost man
Walking through this lonely town
I know that I was born to be great
But I have not shaken the hands of my fate
I know, I have a lot to give
But I'm living in the reality of the unknown man
Nobody knows my name...
but, I'm so good at my game

60.

My Exit

When I Leave the Stage...
Let no tears fall from those I love
For we are called, but a moment to life
And from eternity to death, all that matters
...Was that we gave our best
So, when I leave the stage, may I have but one moment
That I may kiss the lips of death --- for on His back,
I shall take the immortal ride
to the high dimension of the
Everlasting God

About the Author

Roger Cosby, AKA "The Son of Consciousness/New World Poet," is blessed with immense talent, streaming through his veins. As a young child, he grew up as a *wordsmith* and often wrote his thoughts on scraps of paper. As time went on, he realized that those words could be sharp and that they held strong imagery and emotions. Like an arrow, his poetry flies straight to the heart! He is also the author of the published book, "Muhammad Ali, A Champion Supreme in Divine Poetry." www.newworldpoet.org

About the Co-Author

Dr. Kathleen Cosby Tabb writes a blog entitled, "Coffee Cup Devotions," which features inspiring and challenging stories, testimonies, and reflections about biblical truth. She is also the author of a book, entitled "Coffee Cup Devotions with Dr. Tabb" https://www.drkathleencosbytabb. com/ and like her brother, Roger Cosby, AKA" The Son of Consciousness /New World Poet," she has a great love for poetry.

*This book contains the original poems of Roger Cosby, AKA "The Son of Consciousness/New World Poet," with adaptations created by Co- Author, Dr. Kathleen Cosby –Tabb.

Printed in the United States
By Bookmasters